PRAISE FOR

THE BEST MATERIAL FOR THE ARTIST IN THE WORLD

"In the nineteenth century the paintings of Albert Bierstadt brought to canvas and to the world the grandeur of the Rocky Mountains and High Sierra. The poems of *The Best Material for the Artist in the World* by Kenneth Chamlee celebrate the timeless splendor of Bierstadt's work through the witness of many voices and points of view. The poems incorporate the struggles and triumphs of Bierstadt's career as he captured the majesty of the North American continent, bringing us into intimate contact with the art, and the context of family and history in which the unique art was created."

— Robert Morgan, author of *Lions of the West*
and New York Times Bestseller *Gap Creek*

"Kenneth Chamlee's book of poems, focused on a once-forgotten American genius, is itself a work of brilliance and depth. Chamlee offers us his version of a complicated human being set in the context of the world in which he traveled, that included mud and mosquitoes as well as beauty on a heroic scale. Bierstadt left us his vision which endures as both a romantic and a historical account, recorded on room-sized canvases. Chamlee, in turn, gives us a standing portrait of the man. His poems are sober, evocative, and respectful, and they overflow with their own penetrating light, illuminating both the man and an era of exuberant expansion when the vast, wild western half of North America was being claimed and was beginning to be lost."

— Bob Ross, author of *Billy Above the Roofs*

"Kenneth Chamlee's *The Best Material for the Artist in the World* is certainly **the** poetic biography of the remarkable painter Albert Bierstadt. The fifty-one beautifully voiced poems bring him, his contemporaries, the West, and our notions of the man and his work to full illumination. I read the work three times, once out loud. I felt caught up in Bierstadt's thrill of Westward travel and his marvelous descriptions of land and people and his promise. This is a fantastic arc of a life; all the high and low points are here. The final poems, especially the poet's impressions, bring the arc full circle."

— Bob Joly, Director, St. Johnsbury Athenaeum

Also by Kenneth Chamlee

If Not These Things

The Best Material for the Artist in the World
Albert Bierstadt: A Biography in Poems

Kenneth Chamlee

STEPHEN F. AUSTIN STATE UNIVERSITY PRESS

ISBN: 978-1-62288-948-8

Cover Art: Albert Bierstadt. *Looking Up the Yosemite Valley* (1863-75).
[oil on canvas]. The Haggin Museum, Stockton, California.

Production Manager: Kimberly Verhines
Book design by Sandra Carranza
Author photo by Juls Buckman

For more information:
Stephen F. Austin State University Press
P.O. Box 13007 SFA Station
Nacogdoches, TX 75962
sfapress@sfasu.edu
www.sfasu.edu/sfapress
936-468-1078

Distributed by Texas A&M University Press Consortium
www.tamupress.com

For Teresa, who believes

Albert Bierstadt, 19th-century landscape painter of the American West, immigrated to the United States from Germany with his parents in 1832, apprenticed in Europe as a young man, and upon return established himself with the Hudson River artists of New England. He made several extensive tours of the West where he found the subjects that defined his career, one that ranged from great success to bankruptcy. In disregard at his death, interest in Bierstadt's work revived in the 1960s and continues today.

Contents

I. A POISED BRUSH

II. THE WHITE WICK OF DREAMS

III. 'NOWHERE ON HEAVEN OR EARTH'

IV. A BENEDICTORY SKY

Titles in italics are ekphrasis renderings of paintings with the same name.

I
A Poised Brush

BECKONING

From our roof I watched whaling ships
and merchantmen come and go, black masts
with cloudbanks of canvas. We had sailed
on *Hope*, a ship bound from Rotterdam
to New Bedford, father said, to chase
his cooper's trade. I was two and don't
remember, but I grew up smelling
pitch and fish, play harpoon a sharpened
stave stabbed deep in grassy humps of dunes.
For hours I would sit and sand-trace
the maze of rigging on anchored brigs.

In the shop I'd watch my father shape
the barrel staves, pulling the drawknife
over and over, a beckoning,
then magic as he set the first hoop.
I'd guess what each barrel might contain—
beer, potatoes, dried beef outward bound,
salted cod or sperm oil coming home.
He built round pockets of harbor air
and smoothed them, certain and watchful,
while I walked my fingers down my sides
counting my ribs, waiting to be filled.

SHAW'S FRAME FACTORY ON PURCHASE STREET

Wrong flex—and for a slow
second a black scar crawls
my face and widened eyes
before the rainfall crash.
I mind splinters less than
a cold mirror's crack, but
Mr. Shaw swears at me,
calls me stupid German
and docks my pay.

I like the oil paintings
better (they don't shatter!),
each one a world away
from here: a warm Cotswold
farmhouse; marble ruins
gleaming white and ageless;
a green Swiss vale below
ghosted threads of glaciers
fraying from the snowline.

'EVERY PICTURE WORTHY OF A FRAME'

advertisement for painting lessons, age 21

I will lift from your hands
faces of dear husbands
outbound on a whaler,
a sullen girl twirling
her parasol, full dress
sweeping crushed shells and sand.
Together we can limn
a castle from bones banked
at wharfside. Will you try?
Good, then. Surprise yourself;
pin your canvas, open
the paint jar, dip the brush
lightly, your hand just so,
and shape a line from here
to Europe's gold salons.

DISSOLVING VIEWS: NEW BEDFORD AUDITORIUM

The whole hall gasps when one season yields
        to another— Niagara's green rush
whitens to winter's iron; hayfields blink
        from wavegrass to rows of golden ricks.

I thought I'd make a crumb of money
        with Harvey's 'Atmospheric Landscapes,'
watercolors transferred to glass then
        shown with limelight and magic lantern.

Staid portraits and the peeling lectern
        have been set aside. Twenty-five cents
per seat, half again for printed gloss—
        the room hums and a line curls outside.

Eighteen feet wide—the projection stuns
        with its tinted charms: Newport Harbor
at owllight, proud boys with their day's catch,
        but as the slides exchange people thrill

with a bewilderment that burbles
        into laughter—a Puritan church
rides a raft downriver, a sleigh's path
        cleared by strong men chopping a lighthouse.

Mutable truths and spectacle sell.
Booked for two more nights. Then, Providence!

FIRE

Henry Bierstadt walks his son to the harbor,
November 1853

Not to shape barrels, build ships or
chase whales, and I knew that, the walls
in his room lapped with color studies
and sketches. He will learn it is one thing
to pretty the world, another to purpose it.
His brothers think it grand to trace a dream
since they leave the woodshop to follow
some traveler's camera-box all about
New Bedford, making images of harpooners
and widow's walks—graven images
to me—brittle, acidic copies of what
our eyes more clearly see.

He kissed his crying sisters, told Mother
he would be with family, but it is twenty years
since we fled the imperial remainders—
no work, nearly starving, two children
dead already, one not a month before we sailed.
Albert does not remember Anne. Who in Solingen
will remember him?

Now another Napoleon has grasped the empire's helm.
Will it be different? Last week the boys set that camera
on its prop of three legs thick as musket stocks.
"Papa, come look!" they said, and raised the black
drape above the glass for me to bend and see.
But I would not. I have seen the world upside
down, in darkness, and could not look again.

What is a blessing?
He stood there waiting with a thin smile,
holding his simple kit and all that fire.
I took my son's shoulders and turned him
toward the dock.

FIRST CROSSING

I am learning sea-love, its whispers
and lulls, nudge of wind, spray-quickened face
and a stern sky ablaze. But this love
rips wave troughs deep as Berkshire ravines,
throws spears of lightning and passengers
to the rail gripping cleats and rag dreams
as water sweeps away all that is
loose, like prayers of the just-converted.

Mid-passage is a blank, sketchless gray;
trifling swells shrug by with lips of foam
as quietly as milk-whiskered cats.
Will my teacher think me apt or rude?
I left my close world, my brothers' jokes,
Mother wound with worry I would drown,
be pressed into the Dutch navy, or
worse, wed a Methodist and defect.

Nimble crew jump at pipes and whistles
to stow the jib, unhook a fouled line,
their every swing and step gauged for risk
in the rigging tied as seine for stars.

DUSSELDORF, WHITTREDGE'S STUDIO

Hasenclever died before young Albert's
boat had docked. A pity, his mother's cousin.
Whom is he to study now? He asserts
Achenbach will take him, but there's no reason
beyond two mugs to think such boon. His sketches
lack the style of the Academy;
they've promise but no feeling for it. The best is
ordinary. I fear Andreas will flatly
turn him down. But if we tell the boy
Achenbach refuses pupils, then we
can give a corner to him here, employ
him in a proper course, and wait and see.
He may prove apt, Emanuel. He came
with nothing but a letter, did he not?
That speaks a firm resolve; he may yet claim
the skills he wants. We did; have you forgot?

WESTPHALIA WALKABOUT

Near Limburg I met a Bäuerin
carrying on her head a basket
big as a washtub, stuffed with dry leaves
for livestock bedding. She asked if I
had seen her son sent downstream to fish.
I had passed him, yes, feet lolled across
a beached dory, asleep in his red
workshirt, basket empty and fish traps
dry on the rack. "Dummkopf!" she muttered
and turned with a scowl dark as cloudthreat.

I could walk to Teutoburger Wald
and would never want for scenes to paint:
beets and cabbages in the stone-tiered
gardens, low washing docks on the streams,
clothes draped over a woven fence, sheets
neatly spread to dry on crisp stubble.

Outside Muenster I rode standing up
with a farmer as manure dribbled
through the gapped tines of his cartsides.
I shared with him a few oil sketches
of thatched cottages, hayracks mounded
by cheery men and their hale, blond sons,
half-timbered mills with sheaves stacked as high
as a horse. I chopped firewood and slopped
his pigs. Later his wife brought fresh milk
and a trencher of brown bread and cheese.

Some days I roam many carefree miles,
painting where I will, breathing air sweet
with hay and turned earth. Other days I
loiter with lost cows and mark the slope

of cottage roofs, the different browns
redolent of mud, bushes, and trout.
One night I slept in an open field
beneath elms overlooking the Ruhr.
A rumbling cart woke me and I waved
at the farmer but he turned away—
he must have thought I was a gypsy!

Everywhere I stop to sketch I see
castle ruins on a distant tor,
their gray emptiness sad and stately.
I think of their silent keeps, the lost
stories, roofless halls now glossed with dust
and birdlime. And many afternoons
the clouds drop from their hot attics
and throw down heavy quilts of rain.

IN THE FOOTHILLS (Early Effort in Perspective)

Old farmers whittle their lies in the cool
of a collapsing shed, the far post
bowed like a peddler's leg. Chickens and piglets
worry the door of a root cellar damp
with potatoes and fusty onions.

The eave of a half-thatched roof hangs above
a man hunched elbows to knees on a milkstool.
Is he thinking about gapped planks in the
unhinged door? Exposed wattles like a
skeleton found in crumbling plaster? Maybe the wicket
warping by the fence where his wife hangs laundry.
He is too tired or daunted even to wave
at neighbors passing in a cart. Come from town,
a man leads a blinkered horse while his wife
and daughter, hands in their ample laps, don't
wave either, sitting as straight as the muddy ruts that lead

all lines out of the picture—roof cant,
fence-juncture, oblique of trees and wagon bed—
lines drawing eyes from the neglected farm
into sidewoods where they drift to a summit
topped with ruins of another castled baron.

LIMITATIONS OF LANDSCAPE PAINTING

Muscles rippling on the dray Belgian
raise biting flies and haydust, his back
a raft of trembles, tail splashing rump,
ears twitching like crickets.
                            Water chutes
toward the millwheel, swiftbrushing the boards'
mossy velvet as it slicks and fills
each falling bucket, spills
                            to the creak
of leather belts and gears, rumbling wheel,
smell of meal and wet stone, silver quick
fingerlings in the tailrace—
                            and still
this latticed damselfly, a poised brush.

LETTER TO MRS. BIERSTADT FROM
THE MALKASTEN CLUB

The doubts declared in the New Bedford paper
are unfounded, madam, and unjust. Your son
has ample talent and will prove, not later
but sooner, that our witness given as one
mind today is a quite unneeded credit.
We attest to his ethic and industry, have seen
works that warrant for him name and profit,
and any ignorant aspersions are but mean.

While initially we couched our praise
until his skills were meet, you may be sure
young Albert has acquired an artist's ways.
The studies from his summer's ranging tour
are solid proof. We write to insure he gets
his due. Sincerely,
                              Your son's advocates.

SWISS AFTERNOON

Sketch boxes set on a narrow slab,
we dangle our boots over the blue
of Lake Lucerne. This rock bridge is all
that joins Brunnen to the high grazing,
and quickened light requires we stop
to paint glowing sails of homeward boats,
the village spire white as a struck match,
fence-shadows slowly combing pastures.

"Whittredge, have you ever seen it so?"
But for answer, rock-clattering, then
behind him, all bells and brambled wool,
village goats whose bridge we momently owned.
"The *light*," I say, as hill-troughs darken
and a distant window sparks. "The goats
will have to wait." We paint in a rush—
a shaken bell, twice, and suddenly
the lead goat leaps Whittredge, touches, then
vaults me—a double flourish as deft
as any living master's brushstroke.

Now the air is full of flies and dust
and dung-smell, bell clappers and hoof-clicks
as each goat follows the rump in front,
scattering our rimmed twilight as they
amble the grassy slope to Brunnen.

LOST SKETCHBOOK

I re-step the miles to Paestum, white
with glare and rubble, sun stinging like
the devil's breath on Vesuvius
where we sketched like madmen in the smoke

and sulfurous rim-glow, having walked
from Naples at midnight, cooking eggs
and pancetta in the fumaroles
while drinking our Lachryma Christi.

Under every withered bush I look
for its blemished leather, brown as bricks
in the fish market where sharks and rays
slapped at the feet of haughty tourists,

tables slick with waste and prismed scales.
What we have seen this month! Virgil's tomb,
the Blue Grotto, storm clouds off Massa
stacked like coffers of dark prophecy.

Did it fall from my knapsack? Did I
leave it in that dim trattoría
raucous with salty lies and worn swash?
It may well be a workday trophy

in some clammer's outstretched hand, who walks
and stops, peers over the book, then cries
"Look! Here he sketched the Faraglioni!"
before ripping leaves to start his fire.

BOATS ASHORE AT SUNSET

Fishermen have turned the tall fins of their sails
toward home. Some row the last few waves to shore
as a line of men leans into the weight of today's catch,
heaving the nets home with a call-and-pull.

It looks as though they have pulled the wrinkles
out of the sea, straining backwards as
the last wave tucks and flattens to the beach.
Every night they pull the boats ashore, pull down
the twilight scrim, pull shadowed mountains
into the drowse of the sea.

They have pulled the wind ashore too,
where it rests wrapped in the sails till tomorrow,
some of it taut to the mast, some of it
folded below the thwarts where it
breathes softly, rocking the boats.

II
The White Wick of Dreams

SURVEYOR'S WAGON IN THE ROCKIES

The lone figure fifty yards beyond wagon and resting team
cocks arm to hat to shade his disbelief. How can those mountains,
blue and humped as plowed earth, grow taller every day but not closer?

No tripod or transit set, horizon unmarked by boulder,
tree or water's glint. How do you measure a measureless land,
a land empty of everything but wind and grit?

Of five mules and a saddle horse, not one drops its head to graze.

'THE BEST MATERIAL FOR THE ARTIST IN THE WORLD'

Albert Bierstadt joins the Overland Trail
Survey Party, South Pass Route, 1859

I.

Two dollars to sleep on a thin tick
sharing a floor with snoring gold fools!
Pike's Peak crazed Missouri with dreamers
and thieves, but we were the road builders
and hundreds waited to sign each day.
Anxious to paint mountains and skies, I
quit St. Jo after the grand send-off
and walked up to meet the survey team.
At Troy the wintered mules were phlegmy
and gaunt; they could not have pulled a cart,
certainly not our army wagons
with months of provisions, tack and tools.
Colonel Lander fumed and wired for more.

Now the long train drags slowly forward
like a snake humped with an outsized meal.
Storms boom and raw roadcuts churn into
deep mires of sucking mud that pop spokes
from their iron-banded wheels. Lander whips
the struggling mules as if rage alone
could move them. Only five miles some days.
Other days the prairie hums and sways
in easy undulations. The green
whirr and shush soothe me, but the day's heat
fires the night's riot and fierce storms rake
our tents and lift them like sails. Entire
reservoirs of rain gully our camps,
river away bedrolls and pots. Then
mosquitoes rise from the bluestem, haze
us in a singing smoke of needles.

II.

During rests I fix our camera
on its heavy legs, tedious box
of glass and acids, making silvered
plates of timid Shoshone children,
women patting meal by their lodges.
A camera is a type of truth
but stereographs cannot convey
like bold sketches—such exquisite dress!
Shouldered blankets red as a blood moon,
fine necklaces of bear claws and quills.
Some warriors will pose with a clutch
of arrows, but others are afraid
to see faces form on gray paper
like spirits enthralled in heavy mist.
Still, I did not expect the tatters
and beggared faces of children who
stare at our swell of wagons knotted
with barrels and larder kept for trade
and favor with other tribes and posts.
Impassive eyes track our every task.

III.

During my errant apprenticeship
in Westphalia, a dim alehouse
or an opened home never seemed but
a few miles or hours from the last.
Parish churches, common as mullein,
rose toward the same sky as wrecked castles.
Often I would hear the Kyrie
when I passed by at vespers, seeking
the cool of a twined ravine, a strewn
ashlar as the day's dinner table.
Now, westward, each wearing mile reveals
a stark distinction—America

is as raw as a poorly-shod foot.
Towns and stores are shade-rare and ranches
days between. The fickle Platte, at times
a muddy drudge, will suddenly rush
down tiers and tumbles of stones broken
like bombarded walls. Cattle and sheep
wandered German roads but a hundred
thousand bison block our way for hours,
flooding north in a tide of flies and
bellowing. After our mess, the wolves'
unholy songs edge us to the fire
and the hard comfort of our rifles.

One wavering noon a purple braid
runs the hem of the horizon. Day
after day it reweaves itself till
the plains buckle like a parlor rug.
Behind timbered foothills, gray mountains
jag upward, ice-topped and teased with clouds.
The dull Berkshires are groundlings to these
Titans, rising to European
majesty, our western Dolomites!
Everything in me is tingling now—
my hands are forks of Kansas lightning,
my brush galvanized with the power
to suspend antelope in swift chase,
hold deer wary to a storm's menace.
I gather encampments of tepees
along the Wind River and ground them
against the backdrop range. Each day is
a race with dwindling light. I may run
out of millboard and oils but not scenes.
Hills drop-terrace into gravel shoals
shadowed by willow and cottonwood.
The great distances, glazed thin by day,

suffuse rose-orange in twilight's dust.
In my studio, these sketches will
spark memory as I paint the West
I feel—limitless, unreckoned, new.
Polite frames will not suffice—I need
easels hewn from seasoned oak hefting
canvases wide as a wagon's span!

IV.

After South Pass, our small party leaves
Lander's crew to its shovels and sweat
and puts the blue Wasatch to our backs.
We follow a free regress, stopping
where we want, shooting grouse and rabbits,
sketching, writing letters, enjoying
our lives immensely until the game
vanishes, then our supplies. Hungry,
seeking the Big Blue and Wolf River,
we keep painting though we are reduced
to water and flour, no leaven
to make a biscuit. At last we ride
upon a trappers' camp, nothing but
a shallow cave's green-scabbed overhang,
though the stew and whiskey are welcome.

Miles north, a massive prairie fire glows
like a pulsing forge reddening night,
reminding me while we mend brushes
Church has brought volcanoes and jungle
to a draped gallery in New York.
His *Andes* allures a public keen
to peer beyond the fringe of rumor
and share a claim. Viewers parse the scene
with tubes like glassless telescopes,
scouting each circlet's story, lost in

equatorial air, fancying
birdcall, nameless flowers' scent and sway,
but how much more they will want to see
our country's snowcaps and cataracts,
buffalo and lodgepoles seen from bluffs.
His tropic patent is now my spur—
I will stand the Rocky Mountains high
on Broadway and invite all the world.
The tingle in my hands redoubles—
I lift a brand from our campfire, coax
its red nib, then sweep my initials
toward the lacework of stars above me.

FITZ HUGH LUDLOW'S IMPRESSIONS OF THE PLAINS

Bierstadt brought New York writer Ludlow, author of
The Hasheesh Eater, *on his 1863 western expedition to*
chronicle their adventure and to post regular dispatches.

I. Reverse Lightning

A yellow claw jumps ground and grabs
the tail of a downbolt, like an eagle
razoring inverted sky.

Stunned pupils are one second
round as bowls in the touchless dark, then
pinched to sand grains by a shattering sun.

We ride dazed, deafened, soaked,
waving our hats and hallooing
our nonsensical joy.

II. Prairie Lesson

No barrister's bloat in chancery court
was ever as circuitous as this warpery of draws
and bends, muddy feints and failures, as I track
this illogical creek with its preposterous banks
and insufferable gullies. Vexed with dry canteen
and humbled horse, I need a Bactrian mount
under this sun scourging like a Pharaonic overseer.

I clamber and slip, cannot grip any position
to sort my surroundings beyond a hundred feet away.
I am lost in the labyrinth, Minos' multicursal doom,
engine of jealous gods devised to thwart—Oh!
here's our camp. They say
they haven't moved it.

III. Traveling Nebraska

Slabs of anthracite seem a coveted settee
to the seats of an Overland Stage.
One day out of Omaha, two stations away
from the shameful agent who promised
our comfortable delivery, we are not passengers
but freight, insensible commodities
spatulaed into a proximate conjugality,
trying to remain motionless lest any stretch or
spasm be misconstrued, but impossible
in such Inquisitional conveyance.

With each unwashed addition,
begrudged adjustments of long-numb limbs
wring our sedimentary seating into a twist
of Bombay contortionists. Dust and sand
powder our every pore and fiber till we appear
planks of breaded cod layered in a fishwife's pan.
The dream of stretching one's legs seems
a fantasy beyond Paradise, horizontal sleep
a memory pillowed with bitterness.

To keep from pitching into facing passengers,
I secure a rope around my head and shoulders,
passing it through the coach's doors.
As a sleepless blear subdues, I grow less
and less concerned that a hard jostle will
jerk my apparatus into a garrote.
Should any rider roused from stupor notice,
none would interfere.

ENOUGH

Fitz flares words the way a campfire sparks,
meteoric glints and gone, more
luxury than light when all is told.

The muleteer wants to cave his skull
with a cold skillet and fry his brains,
hear the fat words sizzle as smooth oil
pools, then spoon it to a tin, save it
to work the weathered reins and traces.

He says this without looking away
from the fire's mesmeric snap. Too close,
coyotes yammer at a blanched moon.

PAINTING FROM LIFE

Our scout has shot a bull
the size of a wagon
and turns him back and forth
with feints and quick twists
of the reins while I set
my stool, cock umbrella
against the glare, and paint.

This lone bison has stamped
a wheel of blood and dust
large as a tower clock's
face; the brute stands his point,
charging each horse's dare
with an outward lunge and
short check from point again.

I work quickly, paint box
balanced on my lap while
holding the palette up—
eye to bull, brush to board,
sketch secured and satcheled.

'Gentlemen,' I say, 'please,
if you will,' and I wave
my hat at his flared eye.
He jerks toward me and they
fire a volley that would
keel a ship; he does not
fall but takes several
great racks of air, charges,
collapses, rises, then
at last pitches over
and sinks to our mercy.

FIRST VIEW—CHICAGO LAKES

Sleet needles past my fastened collar
as we rise into the house of rain.
Mr. Byers of the *Mountain News*
has horsed us up this flyspeck path
with avowals of Alpine views but
now is silent. I think he has missed
the spur trail. My blood is gelid,
fingers numb beyond recovery.
Clouds tickle and drip and when we crest
this timbered ridge I will ask that—Oh!
Sublime cirque! The Alps surpassed again!
Stay the mules—I must—I need my paints,
stool. Fifteen minutes, please you; see how
the near lake mirrors the breaking storm
with light fine as milkweed fluff, that one
pearled peak soft as the edge of heaven!

SACRIFICE

I saw war's stark harvest
in Brady's photographs
last autumn in New York.
I stood before Watkins'
grand Yosemite prints
and felt our nation's blood
pulsing with a new dream
of Eden and knew when
hell was sheathed we would want
to see it, to own it.

That first fall Leutze and I
rode down to see Edward
at the Potomac camps
where he stereoscoped
visitors and confused
officers' retinues.
It was all brass and blue
uniforms and too much
swagger. That is gone now.

Gifford and Whittredge went
the first month to enlist.
Will be over quickly,
we all said; that was two
years ago. The papers
here in California
say I have been drafted,
my number pulled out of
the pool at Fifteenth Ward.

I will have an agent
dispose the matter through
a commutation fee.
Three hundred dollars—not
one tenth of a painting.

YOSEMITE—TWO MONTHS AFTER GETTYSBURG

We have decamped from the green meadow
three miles back and set our tents along
the Merced where Cho-looke cannons down
and sunset kilns the voiceless rocks.

Before dawn our company troops out
with umbrellas, camp stools and canteens,
paint boxes and bottles of thinner.
All eyes search the valley for good ground,
a place to pitch shade and fill a sheet
that will hold the colors of the field.

At dusk the billets are neatly stacked;
venison simmers in the kettle.
Around the camp, glistening with daubs
of red and black beginning to dry,
our day's work lies spread out in the grass.

FITZ HUGH LUDLOW'S IMPRESSIONS OF THE WEST

I. Swimming in the Great Salt Lake

Black Rock Ranch

We mince across crystal splinters to water's edge,
a few self-mortifying feet of Utah penance.
Wading a quarter-mile to our knees, each step
stirs the unctuous bed and bubbles up
a stench and swirl black as Pluto's realm.
It is not a swim but a buoyancy, not even our ears
dip the pickle bath when splayed on our backs.

In the kitchen, stiffened by our brackish casts, we loom
a colonnade of ghosts. If not his paintings, the artist at least
preserved, brined and ready to be barreled. Eyes and skin
burning, we twist, desiccating by the second,
until the laughing cook unbuckets his rinse
and we dissolve again into men.

Jesus shames the wife who turned toward
burning Gomorrah, reproving her glance as worldly.
Are regret and pity sins as well? Who is strong enough,
looking back, to never mourn?

II. Alkali Plain

Thirteen men in a stage meant for six.
The flats are white hot, as if suspended in the strike
of a phosphorous match, yet waveringly clear,
earth stretched for miles like a wrinkleless pall.
We see the smoke of Cañon Station before rounding
the draw, its main house a reeking pyre—six mutilated men
and a dozen butchered stud, all the hay burned, the water fouled.

There is no help. When the stage jerks away
rifles bristle from the coach and across its top

34

like cactus spines. Our throats are knotted with thirst
and the only sounds are battering hooves
and the wheezing of lathered, white-eyed horses.

III. Eden *In Situ*

Desperations of the desert yield to a green
and scented seduction. California
is an extravagant host—surfeit of figs
and all vegetables, its libertine sun, such ardent
amity from Starr King and Galen Clark, and none of it
a lamina masking some Young or Rockwell,
no citizenry confined or ciphered in its faith.

From Mariposa on strong horses and fine-tooled
saddles to the grove of preposterous trees.
Arms spread and grasping hands, a dozen men
cannot circle one girth, but what a lovely
embrace: the sequoias' rich sienna bark,
their ancient chars, trees a millennium tall
before the humble rood of Calvary.
Realistic rendering proves impossible, proportion
uncapturable on canvas.

Through the portal of gods we enter the vast
granite enclave. Now words demean as well,
wonders beyond metaphor curve to a cleft-dome
terminus, tiered waterfalls spill all around.
We make beds of cedar boughs and from my blankets
the artist routs a rattlesnake and kills it—
auspice or portent I have yet to learn.

IV. Bête Noire

One night's board in a doll bed enlivens
a season of fleas. Morning's gruel and chorusing
hounds enhance our good riddance. When we reach

the Sacramento we learn the extortionate toll to ferry
the artist's color box upriver—freight charged by the pigment.

Starving Diggers and their gnomish women seem
lost to modernity, sad scavenger tribe only one river day
yet a century from the Dog Creek band that trades
fine mink quivers and handsome baskets.
The artist's dresser now strains our party's wagon as we
scrap through chaparral and pitch-pine to reach
Eureka, then follow a foggy coast sentineled
with boulders and firs leaning in with secrets.

One morning my chest weighs heavy as an iron stove lid
and scalds with every serrated cough. A week's
restoration in the care of a solicitous farmwife
leaves me still too weak to mount, so a second week
conveyed in our wagon, shamed like a knight in a cart,
mere dunnage in the straw against the dark wardrobe
of tinctures and chromes. Why will the infatuate artist
not forsake this impedimenta for a pencil and
sketch paper? What loss to bleed Mt. Shasta
until properly studioed and there infuse
the greens and beiges and blues?

I think we will be dragging this mammoth portmanteau
to the Dalles then down the Columbia, racing to catch
the storm-chased steamship before it leaves us
trapped like our own Fort Clatsop with nothing to eat but oils.

WHAT NOT TO PAINT

        green sky and fist-sized hailstones
     boot-sucking mud and broken spokes
skin-singeing sandstorms

rattlesnakes singing at the river ford
        wagons keeled and wheeling air
                gray faces of the drowned

                drunks with pistols, rope justice
        burned-out station houses
red caps of the scalped

the keening fog of mosquitoes
        corn meal squirming with weevils
                immigrant trains turning east

                a vast chapel of carcasses
        silent choir of buzzards
a hundred million buffalo bones

EMIGRANTS CROSSING THE PLAINS

Everything draws toward the white wick of dreams:
a wagon train pushing into the flare
of afternoon; the slow, silty river flanking
redrock cliffs that step down
and down into distance; even a bit of path
opened by a fallen tree arrows into the light.

After a day's dust and rumbling, drovers
lash tired oxen toward a shallow ford and shade.
Soon the party will rein up and build fires
to cook beans and grouse, let sheep muddle
as cows drink and lag. A quick rest,
a morning hail, and the rutted miles again.

There is not much to deter: an abandoned cookstove,
a bison skull and scattered bones, a few black wings
drifting the distant Indian camp.

III
'Nowhere on Heaven or Earth'

WITNESS

Artists Francis Seth Frost and Henry Hitchings
accompanied Bierstadt on his first western trip in 1859.

We ate the same dried beef and beans he did
past South Pass to the Wasatch, got just as drenched
in Kansas downpours, too. We set our stools
and sketched light so sweet and clear you could
pour it on your paper like Vermont syrup.

Five years older, his pupil briefly, I earned
a landscapist's name in Boston while he
tramped Europe practicing craft, earned
good reviews too before his Tyrols and Capris
began to show in New Bedford galleries. I auctioned
a hundred paintings, nearly every one I had,
to range with him and Henry, left my wife and babies
for five months because I wanted to blaze too, we all did,
but he burned an uncommon candle.

After that trip, Henry and I showed some in Boston,
sold a few but never felt the tug to return. We knew
he would because he brought a wagon-load of West
back with him—buffalo skins, painted hides,
beaded shirts and hatchets—and soon had them hung
in a new Manhattan studio where reporters pressed for stories.
Four years I worked to make a show of my western best:
tepee villages near Fort Laramie, Green River on the Fourth
when eight hundred Shoshone rode in with Chief Washakie.
Just before his second trip, with a hired writer now
to tout their travels, *Lander's Peak* left his easel, and
a breeze filled his sails that whipped into a whirlwind
blowing him across the continent and Atlantic
so often we lost count. When we went west the talk
was all Frederick Church; now it was Albert Chartres.

41

Critics complain his paintings are too big—a silly thing
when the widest view they know is the Hudson
facing Hoboken. If his oils were cycloramas they would
not be overdone for breadth. Yes, his grandest mountains
are too tall; we never saw that. But in the canvasses where
the feast of land lies along Wind River like a green
tablecloth peppered with ten thousand buffalo beneath
a sky flame-dancing rim to rim—tell the critics
we saw that. We all saw that.

SCHEMA

"It is better to make shoes or dig potatoes
than seek the pursuit of art for the sake of gain."
—Asher Durand

Wealthy men understand formula.
Let the bear lumber to the lakeshore;
mallards will rise in a high circle,
then plane down to a blue surface smooth
as foyer tile, deer mute as servants.

Waterfalls in the middle, mountains
to the rear, a warrant poets learn
in the posing of a sonnet: lake
rhyming sky, rugged cliffs pairing trees,
mountains measured into stanzas, then
a gemmed couplet of granite and ice.

PATRONAGE

Twenty-five thousand ought to by God buy me grandeur,
something fit for the halls of Collis P. Huntington.
My Central Pacific Railroad blasted nine tunnels
through solid rock to cross the Sierras, kept working
in the winter of '66 without stopping once.
What we did is an engineering marvel, yes sir.

And this? This is what I get? A picture with no train?
I walked that gent to the very dent in Donner Pass
I wanted him to paint from. He stayed night after night,
getting up at four a.m. for the 'right light,' he said.
You think he would have seen one locomotive out there,
maybe a string of Pullman cars hauling for the coast.
Hell, I don't even see any tracks! Just a smoke puff
and a stretch of brown snow sheds stacked against the mountain.

At least he didn't botch it up with some iron horse shit—
coolies and rock piles and burned stumps—and nothing about
that godawful story from the forties we've all heard.
I guess I can live with that. Look at it—he sure does
spread a scene. That lake glows like the Golden Spike, I swear.
But I won't pay it full. Not this way. He'll have to take
less than he wants. Seems fair to me since that's what I got.

CORRESPONDENCE

Rosalie Osborne Ludlow writes to her sister about her husband
Fitz Hugh Ludlow, author of The Hasheesh Eater, *and*
her future husband, Albert Bierstadt.

Esther, you must burn our letters. Promise me.
Put them with that packet twined in ribbon
at the back of the escritoire and throw them
in the stove. It is enough I must divorce that
scoundrel Fitz, but if Father knew of my
letters to Albert he would apoplect.

You were right. Mother was right. I should have
known better than to marry glamour, but
Fitz was lightning and I was struck. He cracked
New York like a thunderbolt—the parties,
the promise! But the acrid blight of his habit
persisted and bred. He acquired vices the way
men keep collars—several at the ready.

When Albert engaged him to follow west and report
I was thrilled. A job! He wrote such splendid letters
to *Golden Era* about the harrowing stage trip and
Yosemite's bliss. But I heard about his postured illness,
the prolonged recovery among doting matrons
from Sacramento to Portland. And now this latest horror
with a Mrs. Ives in St. Joseph, registering her as his wife!

Albert is so sweet. He wrote how I had been deceived
and what I now deserved, all the tenders and insinuations
I told you about. Everything will be proper soon enough
but must appear subsequent to my husband's depravity.
Father must never learn of our preemption. Burn all
the letters, Sister, please, then this one. *Promise.*

THE UNVEILING

Storm in the Rocky Mountains—Mt. Rosalie

February 1866

I want to live in a home, not a realm, not
an acme of unreachable ice, even if my name
flags the pinnacle in resplendent light.

Society hives to each Great Picture—women
in tendrilled, conservatory hats, men in tails
leaning on wolf-head canes. Lifting lorgnettes

to wrinkled noses, they extort secrets from
shadow and sheen, appraise wooded slopes
and the bounty of fleeing Indians, then judge

if the appellation is worthy of its summit
or even its warp of green drapery
shouldering the gilt-leaved frame.

Fitz and Albert told me of a vista unwrapping
after rain, a zenith happily named for absent wife
and friend. Who knew three years of rumor

and deflection would lead to this barnside
of crossed trees' intimating X's, stone faces
glowering from above, a deadfall boulder

framed against molten lake. Oh, Albert,
will milling moths not reprove the abutting triangles'
centered glow and gloom, our deepest shadow

slit by a scalene eye? Am I the light
or the heat between? I want to be the waterfall
that wisps away, never touching the ground.

A CRITIC REVIEWS THE BIERSTADT MANSION

A grander display of gaucherie cannot be imagined.
Four floors of styleless stonework encase this artist's barn
blemished by eruptions of gimcrack corbels, paunched oriels,
and a piazza circumscribing like a moat.

Malkasten—*paintbox*—even its name invokes the dull
school of Dusseldorf. He first called it Hawksrest
and should have kept that raptorial sobriquet
as it suits his clawing for commissions. Skins and heads

of dead beasts adorn the floors and walls
of wooden rooms warrened for music, billiards
and books. Racked for review, paintings hedge
a studio the size of a cricket pitch. Such space

could serve six artists, yet defines but one
Teutonic ego. Easels equal to a truss bridge
tilt facile paint-scapes toward towered windows
framing a greened cliffslope to the Hudson.

We hear this house is a gift for his wife-to-be, a wife
still yet another's, even as stories thick as bedroom
tapestries weave from Waterville to Irvington, through
sleepy Tarrytown, then incline to this lording bluff.

EAST COAST SKEPTICS

*"What would they have? I wonder what
they think the sea's like?"* J.M.W. Turner

No mountains can be that tall, they caw.
Clouds cannot amass nor light concoct
such beatific vapors, assert
the longitudinally assured
with voices creaking like scroll-top desks.

COMPOSITION

I'll break my easel into fire-scrap,
knot my brushes into a duster,
then scour the day in Washington Square
listening for gossip rich enough
to gild a plot. From a farmer's limp,
a deacon's leer and jurist's frock coat,
I will meld my hero and pen him
into a sea of inky troubles.
Who would decry his federation?

But if I know yarrow by the Platte,
deer browsing an aspened park at dawn,
nameless peaks jagged as a pike's mouth
and paint them under the massing sky
of a glorious storm they call me
an assembler, a confectioner
false to truth and nature, thus to art.

In New Bedford the sailors all know
Ahab's tale is no biography.
Is he a lie? Forged from injury,
rumor and imagined fire, he rides
his blindness toward every soul's abyss.
Where's truth then, in rigor or in rave?
Ensemble is not pastiche, by God.

CRITICAL DIFFERENCE

No oil is hot enough to boil them,
Rosie, trying to nose-ring people
into a common stall. Jealous goats!
How many years of writing their smudge
would it take Cook and Jarves to earn
what I can make in one commission?
Louis-Napoleon gave to me
the Legion of Honor, and Berlin's
Royal Academy a gold medal.
Do these things matter to no one now?
They fawn over fuzzy splatterings
of mills and flowers, waving sharp pens
in the public's face, yet all the time
clamping monocles in purblind eyes.

No, dear, I will go downstairs and speak
as a gentleman in this matter.
Irritable? Merely their business?
Those guttersnipes? Jackanapes! Triflers!

REDACTED

In his 1870 publication The Heart of the Continent,
Fitz Hugh Ludlow removed every instance
of Albert Bierstadt's name.

How long, I wonder, had his squinting eye apprized my Rose?
From her first visit to his Tenth Street atelier to view
the snowy ensign to poor Lander? From her bon voyage
embrace in Missouri as we began that exhausting, enthralling
trek which I so exquisitely dilated for the *Post*?
I think his calculus was booked when we spied
the vista he induced me to share as "Monte Rosa."

Just three years from that tramp to their marriage. She scalpeled me
like a cyst, turned her parents from me so to have Europe
and a bawdy house in Irvington! Well, the devil all.
This refined assembly of dispatches and *post factum*
expositions will flaunt the true genius of that journey:
my grasp of mineralogy and plants, my objective
dissection of the Mormon curse. People misunderstand
the stem of my enlightenment; what fools impugn as trammels
are but phantasmagoria, prismatic oases
that his dull-colored collages can never hope to find.

Critics have disposed him well. They have censured the scenewright
and his sentimental ostentations, no more sublime
than a sandbar. I cast him nameless, roped to a foundered
reputation. My phoenix will soar from these bright pages
unprickled by the nose of his offense. And as for her,
I wish him all her thorns!

IN YELLOWSTONE, TEN YEARS AFTER
THE HAYDEN SURVEY

The whole world knows this place. Moran learned
from me what I learned from Church—grandeur,
bold lighting, theatrical debut.
His palette proves right, not prodigal
as snipes claimed; he sloped and placed of course,
but what a devil's quarter! Geysers
blast like fireboat hoses; mud cauldrons
belch and steam while chaos seethes below.

What did I miss, staying west with Rose
that year, selling the Valley over
again while Moran crafted his name
to an endurance—First Painter
of the Parks? Yosemite had been
saved for the state—Lincoln signed it—but
a nation's park? That was unforeseen,
so I stayed to scope the Sierras
then foment that grand buffalo hunt
for His Royal Indulgence, Alexis.

Yesterday we rode in as tourists.
We camp where we are told and cannot
hunt though the wide valleys thrive with elk
and bison. Colter and Bridger were
not believed, but Congress paid Moran
for his mélange of falls and canyon,
brightly prismed pools with sulfur's stink.

INVENTORY

My scared nightman swears all fires were cold
when the renters left the day before,
only ashes in the kitchen stove,
no coal in the bedroom grates upstairs,
so what am I to say? Doubt does not
uncrack the delft, unwarp Moroccan
inlay, unchar painted shirts bartered
at Fort Laramie from chary Sioux.

Twenty-two pictures were frenzied out
while the fire wagons struggled uphill.
Memories, though, reduce more slowly
than oak, and in gray boot-swirls above
still-snapping beams and seething gneiss,
I see daylight's quiet grace vesting
the tall windows, knowing how it once
shared the promised *Domes* and *Donner Lake.*

Our grand house is lost yet my wife burns
six years with consumption. Malkasten
raged for a night, lit Hudson Valley
from West Point down to Piermont, and all
came out to gawk and gabble, but, bored
before dawn, they returned to their own
griefs and the short wait for something else
to turn their attention like a bell.

PAINTING IN THE TROPICS

at the Royal Victoria Hotel, Nassau

This island is lush as a prairie,
sand white and soft as June cottonwoods.
Old women in macaw-bright dresses
haggle for plums in the dawn market
as sponge boats set out from the harbor.

Rosie has not come down. She sits with
an embroidery pressed to her mouth
and whispers to her nurse for warmed tea.
She might feel better for the salt breeze
and a sun-chair on the veranda,
or a slow beach walk where the fine shells
crunch like hoarfrost under buttoned shoes,
the bay blue as a field of lupine.

I will sit in bouldered shade, sketching
the afternoon as it marshals waves
into a legion of peaks pushing
shoreward, each billow a greenish pane
as it crests then shatters into spume.

When the light fails I will pass by men
pitching seaweed into ox carts, pass
anchored sloops and steamers, then try to
ignore the sand's pallor, waves lapping
at slack tide like small coughs.

A VIEW IN THE BAHAMAS

Yellow jackfruit hang like moons
over the crab-legged shanty, its doors
open to a look-through breeze.
The ridgeline thatch is pinched with iron bands
against autumn storms, but slender men with baskets
have come from the market with cassava bread
and prawns to share under an untroubled sky.

Everything raises itself to the sun: the blooming cactus,
yucca spiking from its dagger leaves, thumb of lighthouse
over lapis sheen of bay, even the tapered palms
rise like fireworks into green bursts of fronds.

IV
A Benedictory Sky

CHIEF ROCKY BEAR VIEWS *THE LAST OF THE BUFFALO* IN PARIS, 1889

Buffalo Bill's Wild West toured with nearly a hundred
Oglala Sioux as performers. Members of the troupe came
regularly to see this painting displayed in a downtown gallery.

I step into the stillness of the great picture,
touch a dying bull's coarse hair, chant
a death-song for the rider fallen by his gray pony.
Nothing moves, but I smell the dust and dung
of herds filling the far plain as in those
summer hunts when we packed home stripped meat
and hides scraped for robes and lodges.

A bull standing with arrowed side and blood-
bubbled nose stares past me at the grand
trinity fixed in its essential moment—
rearing white horse, warrior with raised spear, bull
thrusting its massive head and horns into the stallion's flank.

I hear the hunters' quick yips, dream
each groan and lunge of the beasts,
remember my grandmother's prayer
but when I step out of the frame
the buffalo are gone and I am
still a Lakota in a painted show.

STRANDED IN ALASKA

At dawn the Tlingit canoes arrived
to fetch us from the grounded steamer.
Cold rain lashed and waves banged the dugouts
into the drum of the pitched hull, but
in the end all was saved but the ship.
We stood there in the mush and gravel
with our boots soaked and nowhere to go
but into the stinking cannery
and the Chinese huts greasy with smoke.

Five days I breathed chum and gagged chowder,
watched eagles fight above the fish-pens,
shrieking and stealing despite the rain.
In the factory Tlingit women
severed fins, heads, and tails in the blade
of a second; insides spilled and scales
gleamed like flakes of rainbow. Reeking vats
drove me out to my umbrella's drip
and patter. I sketched dull scrapwood shacks
with tin roofs weighted by stones, plotted
islands no bigger than scuffs of moss.

The *Ancon* lay close to shore, her length
receding into fog. From the stern
I marked the fatal tilt of the stack
against the offset beam, the yellow
paddleboxes useless and absurd.

I came for a different Alaska,
one that would pay in grand commissions,
the one exalted in tourbooks—where
the captain scouts for orca and names
the passing glaciers. I had wanted

to see their palatial facades crack
and hear them plunge among littered floes
with crushing surge, to see boreal
forests deploying from the coasts for
mile upon impenetrable mile
sweeping up to mountains and ranges
so august the Sierras seem mocked
as pencil stubs.
                But there was only
drench and drab skies, nothing that would pay,
nothing that would pique a nation so
inured to majesty they reject
their own. As I claimed the derelict's
foreshortened view, a Chinese man toiled
his way to my stump. Grinning wide and
jabbering, he raised a pot of tea
and a chipped bowl of pink fish and rice.

WRECK OF THE "ANCON" IN LORING BAY, ALASKA

A hawser cast too early, slack fire
in the boiler—and all is riven.
Ebb tide pulls and the *Ancon*
breaks her keel on a hidden reef, listing
so steeply her starboard sidewheel
is nearly dry, shrugged like a shoulder
to the chill gray sameness of sea and fog.

Fast between two worlds of hope
she leans toward a lightening sky
and the headland she will never round,
yet so close to shore a loud hail
should right her. Knifing out from dark bushes,
a fallen trunk and shoreline merge
to suggest a prow, ghost of a ruined hull
and a long forgotten ore.

SIXTEEN WINTERS

Doctors said warmth and blue waters would
slow the immolation of her lungs,
and New Providence proved a true clock
with palm leaves ticking in a rank breeze.

In Italy I painted boatmen's
prize sole. Near Monterrey, seals and pups.
But when we came here, florid sunsets,
sea turtles scooping past surf-wreckage,
a storm-shattered mast piercing a fringed
breaker's areola of debris.

Today I paint waves part crashing curl,
part gossamer shard mined in the same
jade as her eyes, a green fire only
the sea can know: hurricane heat, volt
of the eel, lambent constellations
of jellyfish, pulsing like grief.

CONVERSATION AT THE UNION LEAGUE CLUB, FEBRUARY 1902

partially quoted from William Howe Downes

He complained of headache
and asked for tea, but when
his attendant returned
he had slumped in his chair.
Did you know him?

                  —No, I

confess not. I had not
heard his name in so long,
I did not know he was
alive until I saw
that he had died.

CONJECTURE

Bierstadt's first western showpiece, Base of the Rocky Mountains,
Laramie Peak, 1860, *loaned by the Buffalo Fine Arts Academy
to a local high school in 1922, was lost and remains unlocated.*

Backdrop for the seniors' jumble of *O Pioneers!,*
this wistful assembly of hunters and bison
bearing six decades of critical shellac is carted
into backstage gloom and pitched against
an abject Veronese balcony where it leans,
obvious and unseen as a middle child

until snickering second-stringers goaded from dare
to prank, spirit the painting to a nearby farm, where
kindled by Tomahawk Ale, they cock the captive
against a haystack and with borrowed pistol
take potshots at their own shadows ghosting
buffalo and Indians illumined by imminent fire.

THE DIRECTOR OF THE MUSEUM OF NATURAL HISTORY ORDERS A BIERSTADT PAINTING DESTROYED

Nine feet by seventeen and quite impossible
to hide—his largest ever to warp an easel.
Ships could sail with less canvas. Ships like
Santa Maria, Niña, Pinta,
holy vessels of *The Landing of Columbus*.

Fifty-one years this flagrance bumped from gallery
to hallway until it beached in the boiler room.
A wedding gift to his second wife,
he had sailed to Spain to learn costume,
even walked the very spot on Watling's Island.

Too dear, she couldn't bear to keep it when he passed,
so gifted us. He seemed to get the details right:
bromeliads and coconut palms,
a white beach curving toward anchored ships,
the native harvest—ripe melons, sea turtle, conch.

It's the rest I can't abide: shadowed Indians,
stunned by the apparition of white gods, bow down
to blazonry and standards, kneel
to a token while gibbered voices
sing Te Deum to errant navigation,
and all around that overly heavenly light
falling from below, behind, above, reddening
the rooted grass and palmy duomo.

Go on; take it. History will write
what it will. I won't become its vaunted savior.

PHOTOGRAPH OF BIERSTADT IN HIS NEW BEDFORD STUDIO

Three bearded followers in formal clothes attend the artist
while he adds ocherish touches to deer
turned toward a coming storm. One monitor
is bald; another braces the wall behind a silk-hatted man
sitting stove-piped and stiff as an antler. But a fourth
flops a leg onto a footstool, crosses his
right boot over and isn't even watching
the assiduous painter but gazes into the studio opposite

at my unshowered, finger-combed head
bowed to a Levenger pad and a favorite Mont Blanc
with which I scribble this morning's notes and wish
the gravel-spreader working the dirt lane beyond our yard
would come back this afternoon so it could
out-ruckus the next-door dogs as they ritually
unglue at 2:10 when our neighbor arrives with her
three pre-school wards, one of whom is
shrieking raw vermilion rips before they reach the front door.

AT THE METROPOLITAN MUSEUM OF ART

American Wing, Room 760

A disapproving docent in black blazer glares as I graph
Bierstadt's massive *The Rocky Mountains, Lander's Peak*
in my point-and-shoot way—snap, a step sideways, snap.
One square at a time, I rescue from dim prints and inadequate books
a dress's beadwork under braided hair, a tended kettle,
claws of a killed bear and faces rapt with a hunter's tale.
I hold the tiny camera above my head to level
the hero's peak, buff of clouds, glacier curving toward central falls.

I smile at the docent and he jerks his radio, hoping
for the shrill of the invisible barrier—*Sir, step back!*
Tall, broad-shouldered, more like a guard but nothing like
the petite, perfumed ancient stationed by the Monets,
he is tired of tour guides extolling the artist-explorer
and his satchel of sketches easeled into this grand compendium
of Indian life. He wants a story for the breakroom, a tale
of intervention and arrest. But I know my limit as I
hold breath, then release, over and over across this canvas
the size of thirty-seven opened coffee table books.
I am here for stories too, close enough now to walk
with the elk hunter's wife who dreams her hands
shaping soft hide to her husband's shoulders, to see
a dog guarding a cradled baby beside a tepee sketched
with seven bold-colored horses, to hear a man with carved pipe
teach his son the weight of smoke. So many stories they

start pushing and spill from the frame, dragging others
from behind, shouting and pointing: it's *Lander's* predecessor,
the lost pendant *Laramie Peak*, known only by reviews and a sidelong
gallery photograph, and here's Bierstadt himself, staging the painting
for a charity fair, big wigwam and natives drumming a Rattlesnake Dance;

68

he refuses ten thousand dollars and sells it for twenty-five
before it tours the States and Europe, and shrilling above them all
the seesawing critics, one gushing *Lander's Peak* is
"unexcelled by any landscape ever painted" and another grouching
"immature, and, on too pretentious a scale," and still

stories are pressing; they scramble this white room claiming
Lander's wall-mates—Church's *Heart of the Andes*
and General Washington being rowed—and now their stories too,
coil like jungle vines and river currents, stories swirling
to the ceiling and down to the floor, back to the feet
of the bored docent ready for his rotation to the Monets,
their simplicity and quiet, the way water lilies remind him
of the label on a bottle of scented oil, and how his wife
smiles as she stands dripping, toweling after her bath.

RENEWAL

The Domes of the Yosemite, 9.5' x 15'(St. Johnsbury Athenaeum), was
removed in October 2017, restored, and returned in July 2018.

The centenarian canvas eases away from its long watch,
edged around its mammoth frame by attendants
mincing like ledge-walkers, then ticks forward
into gloved hands down to a papered floor.
Across its bared back, a Victorian apparatus of hooks
and laces is undone, and now the great uncorseted painting
can lift its corners a bit, stretch an old sag after ages
of holding it in. Patient hands sweep storied dust
and lay out traveling garb. A snug wrap,
a cushioned ride—winter at a spa in Miami.

Next summer, arriving in a tube stout as a Corinthian column,
ends bubbled with red padding, a giant baton passes;
the regent scene is unrolled and reset, its broad
backside firmed by a chic liner, front taut and vibrant.
Gone are mists of age and old varnish, as if you had
climbed to Lower Falls and stood pointing at Royal Arches'
crescent scours, spring melt pounding a cold matte spray
that silks your face—and with a quick swipe
a greyed world dazzles again.

VISION

View from the Wind River Mountains, Wyoming, 1860
Museum of Fine Arts, Boston

Before each whipped Olympus with meringue of clouds,
before commerce glossed his memory, Bierstadt painted
a year of unscaffolded skies and rivers ribboning plains
absent any honorific peak, scenes of casual imprecision

and delight, like this one with its heraldic morning,
thick trees tracking a watercourse through rock towers
down to a topaz verdure, two riders
and a packhorse descending a trail-less slope

carrying a freedom I cannot imagine, carrying
everything they know is enough, a surety
found in those few Wind River paintings
sketched on site but refigured

two thousand miles away, like this one in the museum
built on land once foraged by the Massachusett.
I want to believe this painting affirms ease and choice,
moving light on the land, accepting seasonal gifts,

but by 1860 the removals were thirty years on
and my wish is blind though the painting is bold,
not frosted or sagging like me, and the hill where it was
brushed to beginning today likely faces a green-striped

snake of interstate. Then I see it, what I didn't
see so many times—a thread of faint white dots
mid-valley, right of the river, an unmistakable
string of wagons and teams, tiny as cells.

WALKING THROUGH AN EXHIBITION ON AN EARLY SUNDAY MORNING

"Albert Bierstadt: Witness to a Changing West"
Buffalo Bill Center for the West, June 2018

I. Entrée

Among the carpeted arroyos I find
frames like lucent windows trimmed
in intricate carvings and gilt
bracing vistas and brute portraits.
No one else is here.

A tree in autumn bronze
arches above a skid of rocks
pitching into a lake where three elk
splash through backwater shallows.

> Sidelight graves Yellowstone Canyon
> into seeming bas-relief
> as cloudshreds mirror
> mist off the river with its
> palpable roar.

A nod to each crown
in the Royal Gallery: antelope,
bighorn, mountain goat, moose.

> And now a bison lumbers so close
> his coarse hair scrapes the sill
> as he halts and trains
> a side-eyed stare.

Shoshone women boil roots
as dogs yip at approaching riders; other camps
are breaking down tepees, tying parfleches
as ponies wait for the next long plod.

Without realizing, I have walked up on the artist
working en plein air. In a pane of rough poses
buffalo appear at the end of his brush;
he turns them, stands them, settles them
down, old bulls and cinnamon calves. Then he
draws a green shade, upper left,
and quickstrokes a Native profile,
windworn and cragged.

Some scenes spread like two porch posts
at an overlook hotel—bison fording
beneath a hawkbill moon, bison shouldering
a prairie gale, bison stopped at a riverbank
fired by a benedictory sky.

Strange to remember the blurred vision
of some who look at *The Last of The Buffalo*
and fumble its title, who cannot see
dual fates in the central pillar, see only
a weapon in the hunter's hand
and not the angle of that lance:
same slant as riders pounding in,
same slope as six dead and dying buffalo,
same tilt of six skulls counted from the corner,

or of some who cannot step back and see
the closer triad of fallen horse,
killed warrior and beast, who cannot see
the squared hump of a solitary bison
patterned in a mountain behind
or the back of another bull level
as the mesa above him, who miss every
prima facie parallel of land and living,
and who miss the black hollows of the closest
skull, turned toward the casual viewer.

II. Reprise

Elk

Afternoon candles his rack
and lights his rump. He bugles
to his harem, strange squeaking
like a rip of rusted hinge,
hears no answer from the cows.
Near the river, a young bull
snorts, shakes his mane and paws earth.

Prong-horned Antelope

Four earth-defying legs,
cirrus belly and argent scarf,
a pair of sable heart-curved horns
all heating in afternoon's parch.
Heads lifted by sharp sound or scent,
flight or frolic is all the same—
the love they know is *speed.*

A Bull Buffalo

As dark a mountain as ever shadowed plain,
the great brown hump and shoulder, wild forelock
fill a broadside view, so close you see

the black marble and blood-moon
crescent of his eye, turned
warily, gauging

the artist,
his death-
smell.

No ground beneath them.
Once prairie mud and thunder, now
yellow dust floats them—
ten bulls, two cows, four calves—
hoofless, no place or way to run.
One calf nurses while another bawls.
A resting bull's shagged flank
is torn like the edge of a territory.

Above the token herd a warrior's
disembodied face, fixed gaze
level as the plains, his red shirt
a shouldered grassfire,
swept hair black and starless.

Indians Traveling Near Fort Laramie

Mounted and impatient, the men are pointing
toward the next remove, north, the broken herds.
Dogs snuff among camp bones while women slowly
fold the tepee covers. They will be walking,
babies on packboards, leading tired ponies
humped with bundles that lift the travois' sweep,
twin rakes effacing each mile and stolen home.

An old woman rides a jouncing seat,
telling her granddaughter about distant camps,
cold, swift rivers and deer bedding in the willows.
On the low horizon, a beacon rockspire,
hearth memory for the westward, but one rider
turns and remembers his dream—a lost warrior's
coup stick, stripped of feathers, its notches
scoured away by wind and whipping sand.

MONUMENT

New Bedford Rural Cemetery

Not this slick, stunted thumb of tombstone.
A mausoleum perhaps, a monolith
staunch as a canyon wall, but not this
gessoed stump faced only with two dates
and the glare of opposing graves.

How many people today in the Met, the Haggin,
in Birmingham and New Britain read his name
in a square of wallscript beside Wind River, Seal Rock,
the Sierra Nevada? How many felt they could breathe
sweetgrass, sea spray, incense-cedar and Jeffrey pine?

You have to walk up to the curved stone
to see the letters moused with lichen,
to read the letters chiseled in bold relief
across the arch-top, bearing his name
to the fierce blue vault above.

NOTES

Dissolving Views   English artist George Harvey produced a famous series of American scenery and later toured the eastern United States giving lectures and showing the paintings via a Drummond Lamp. In 1851 he leased the presentation to Bierstadt.

Fire   Bierstadt's brothers, Charles and Edward, both became photographers.

Dusseldorf: Whittredge's Studio   Though never officially enrolled in the Kunstakademie, Bierstadt was befriended by American artists studying there, including Worthington Whittredge and Emanuel Leutze.

Letter to Mrs. Bierstadt from the Malkasten Club   Whittredge wrote that the letter was written in the artists' favorite gathering place and signed by Emanuel Leutze, Andreas Achenbach, William Haseltine, and J. B. Irving.

The Best Material for the Artist in the World   Colonel Frederick West Lander led annual surveys for road-building in the 1850s. In a letter to *The New Bedford Daily Mercury* dated September 14, 1859, Bierstadt wrote: "For the most part, the weather has been delightful, and such beautiful cloud formations, such fine effects of light and shade, and play of cloud shadows across the hills, such golden sunsets, I have never before seen. Our own country has the best material for the artist in the world."

Sacrifice   Photographer Carleton Watkins' large-scale prints of California scenery were on display at Goupil's gallery in New York in December 1862.

Gordon Hendricks wrote in his pictorial biography that Bierstadt's grand landscapes were often composite creations "the like of which existed nowhere on heaven or earth."

Witness   In late 1859 Bierstadt relocated from New Bedford to the famous Tenth Street Studio in Manhattan which housed over its course artists Frederick Church, Sanford Robinson Gifford, Worthington Whittredge, Emanuel Leutze, William Bradford, Martin Johnson Heade, and many others.

Critical Difference   Art critics Clarence Cook and James Jackson Jarves offered Bierstadt qualified praise initially but later wrote harsh and disparaging personal critiques.

Redacted   Col. Frederick Lander died in March 1862 from wounds suffered in battle several months earlier.

Inventory   Bierstadt's magnificent house on the Hudson River was destroyed by fire, November 10, 1882.

Walking Through an Exhibition on an Early Sunday Morning
Two new exhibitions (and attendant catalogues) appeared in 2018: *Albert Bierstadt—Witness to a Changing West* (Buffalo Bill Center for the West and the Gilcrease Museum) and *The Rockies and the Alps—Bierstadt, Calame, and the Romance of the Mountains* (Newark Museum).

ACKNOWLEDGMENTS

I am grateful to the following magazines for the first publication of these poems:

Blueline Magazine—"Dissolving Views: New Bedford Auditorium"

Broad River Review—"Vision"

Cold Mountain Review—"The Best Material for the Artist in the World"

Ekphrasis—"Emigrants Crossing the Plains"

The Ekphrastic Review—"First View—Chicago Lakes" and "Surveyor's Wagon in the Rockies"

Flying South—"At the Metropolitan Museum" and "First Crossing"

I-70 Review—"Painting From Life" and "Inventory"

Library Love Letter: Letters One—"Renewal"

Montana Mouthful—"Enough"

Naugatuck River Review—"The Director of the Museum of Natural History Orders a Bierstadt Painting Destroyed"

North Carolina Literary Review—"Composition"

Ocean State Review—"Sixteen Winters"

Rockvale Review—"Beckoning" (as "Beginning") and "Boats Ashore at Sunset"

Stone Poetry Journal—"Photograph of Bierstadt in His New Bedford Studio"

THINK: A Journal of Poetry, Fiction, and Essays—"Every Picture Worthy of a Frame," "Dusseldorf: Whittredge's Studio," "Westphalia Walkabout," and "Letter to Mrs. Bierstadt"

Twelve Winters Journal—"Fitz Hugh Ludlow's Impressions of the Plains" and "Fitz Hugh Ludlow's Impressions of the West"

Weber: The Contemporary West—"Walking Through an Exhibition on an Early Sunday Morning"

Willawaw Journal—"Stranded in Alaska" and "Wreck of the Ancon in Loring Bay, Alaska"

Willows Wept Review—"The Unveiling" and "Yosemite—Two Months After Gettysburg"

The Worcester Review—"Fire" and "Witness"

"Limitations of Landscape Painting" was published in *A Gathering of Poets* (Jacar Press, 2016).

"What Not to Paint" was published in *Kakalak: An Anthology of Carolina Poets* (Main Street Rag Publishing Company, 2015).

***

Many thanks to Brevard College for the sabbatical and faculty development funding that allowed this project to begin and continue, and to the Hambidge Center for three residencies during its progress.

Thanks also to Billy Collins and the Southampton Writers Conference 2010 poetry workshop for their critique of the initial poems in this project, and to Joan Houlihan and Peter Covino for helpful feedback at the Colrain Poetry Manuscript Conference in Truchas, New Mexico, 2019.

Generous friends allowed me to stay in their homes during museum visits or for extended periods of writing time. Without these gifts, the book would not exist. Heartfelt gratitude goes to Phyllis Langton, Melanie St. Raymond, Mike and Amy Clarke, Earl and Ann Rabb, Peter and Eleanor Mockridge, and Scott Green and Russell Mellette.

The encouragement and feedback from friends and fellow writers was profoundly helpful and greatly appreciated. Many thanks go to Margaret Brown, Jane Curran, Anne Green, Jubal Tiner, and most especially, Karen Jackson and Tonya Staufer.

Finally, for her faithful support and unwavering belief in me and this project, profound love and thanks to my wife Teresa, to whom this book is dedicated.

RESOURCES

I used many excellent sources to create this portrait of Albert Bierstadt, but these were central and significant:

Anderson, Nancy, and Linda Ferber. *Albert Bierstadt: Art and Enterprise.* The Brooklyn Museum, 1990.

Baigell, Matthew. *Albert Bierstadt.* Watson-Guptill, 1988.

Harvey, Eleanor Jones. *The Painted Sketch: American Impressions from Nature—1830-1880.* Dallas Museum of Art, 1998.

Hassrick, Peter. *Albert Bierstadt: Witness to a Changing West.* University of Oklahoma Press, 2018.

Hendricks, Gordon. *Albert Bierstadt: Painter of the American West.* Harrison House, 1988.

Houston, Alan Fraser and Jourdan Moore Houston. "The 1859 Lander Expedition Revisited." *Montana: the Magazine of Western History,* Summer 1999, pp. 50-71.

Ludlow, Fitz Hugh. *The Heart of the Continent.* Hurd and Houghton, 1870.

Robotham, Tom. *Albert Bierstadt.* Crescent Books, 1993.

ABOUT THE AUTHOR

 Author Photo by Juls Buckeman

Kenneth Chamlee is the author of *If Not These Things* (Kelsay Books, 2022) and of two contest-winning chapbooks, *Absolute Faith* (ByLine Press) and *Logic of the Lost* (Longleaf Press). His poems have appeared in *The North Carolina Literary Review, Cold Mountain Review, The Worcester Review, Ocean State Review, Weber: The Contemporary West,* and *The Ekphrastic Review,* among other places. He is Professor Emeritus of English at Brevard College in North Carolina and holds a Ph.D. from the University of North Carolina-Greensboro.